I WONDER Why

The Dinosaurs Died Out

and other questions about extinct and endangered animals

Andrew Charman

KINGFISHER
NEW YORK

Distributed in the U.S. and Canada by Macmillan,
175 Fifth Ave., New York, NY 10010

First published 1996 by Kingfisher

Consultants: Andrew Branson, Michael Chinery,
David Burnie

Library of Congress Cataloging-in-Publication data
has been applied for.

ISBN: 978-0-7534-6953-8

Kingfisher books are available for special promotions and
premiums. For details contact: Special Markets Department,
Macmillan, 175 Fifth Ave., New York, NY 10010.

For more information, please visit www.kingfisherbooks.com

Printed in China.
9 8 7 6 5 4 3 2 1
1TR/0912/UTD/WKT/140MA

Illustrations: John Butler 18–19; Mike Davis 13bl; Peter Dennis
(Linda Rogers Associates) 24–25; Christian Hook 30–31; Biz
Hull (Artist Partners) 28–29; Ian Jackson 12–13, 16–17, 20–21;
Tony Kenyon (BL Kearley) all cartoons (except 13bl); Terence
Lambert 22–23; Alan Male (Linden Artists) 14–15; Nicki Palin
6–7; Maurice Pledger (Bernard Thornton Artists) 10–11; Bryan
Poole 4–5; David Wright (Kathy Jakeman) cover, 8–9, 26–27.

CONTENTS

4   Why are there no dinosaurs on Earth?

4   Do all animals die out?

6   Why is the dodo dead?

7   Which extinct animal looked
    half-horse, half-zebra?

8   How many insects are there?

9   Which endangered insect is bigger
    than a mouse?

10 Why do animals like wetlands?

11 Which orphans are fed by puppets?

12 Why are boats bad for manatees?

12 Where do sturgeon eggs go?

13 Why should you keep olms a secret?

13 How can fish make an eagle sick?

14 Which endangered animal has a
    magic horn?

15 Where can you shoot elephants?

15 Which "extinct" animal returned to
    the wild?

16 Why do orangutans need so many
    trees?

16 Which endangered animal is
    the shiest?

17 Why is it bad luck to be an aye-aye?

17 Which fox flies to its food?

18 Why are polar bears still at risk?

18 Why do seals get their fur dyed?

19 Which threatened whale has a unicorn's horn?

20 What's so "right" about the right whale?

21 Are there parks in the ocean?

22 When do parrots make bad pets?

23 Who carries a chameleon in a suitcase?

24 How could a bonfire save elephants?

25 Who grabs coconut crabs?

25 Why would leopards prefer to not be spotted?

26 Why do tigers need corridors?

26 How does a possum cross the road?

27 Why are gorillas not to be sniffed at?

28 When do animals like going to the zoo?

28 When do animals like leaving the zoo?

29 Which endangered animal is raised in a bucket?

30 Why do animals need us?

31 Why do we need animals?

32 Index

Why are there no dinosaurs on Earth?

Animals can become extinct either because of things people do or because the places they live in change.

The dinosaurs lived on Earth for millions of years. Then around 65 million years ago, they became extinct—every single one of them disappeared. No one knows exactly why, but one idea is that a giant asteroid crashed into Earth. As a result the climate changed, and the world became too cold for the dinosaurs.

Do all animals die out?

Every kind of animal dies out eventually. But new kinds of animals usually appear to take their place. These new species are often descendants of the extinct ones. For example, the elephants on Earth today are related to the hairy mammoths that disappeared around 10,000 years ago.

Many animals are endangered—in other words they are in danger of dying out because people have hunted too many of them or are still hunting them.

When harmful chemicals get into the air, soil, or water, they can cause pollution. This can poison so many animals that the species becomes endangered.

When people move to new parts of the world, they often take animals with them. These new animals sometimes hunt the ones that already live there.

Some animals are endangered because the places where they live are cleared out to make space for farms, factories, roads, or houses.

Why is the dodo dead?

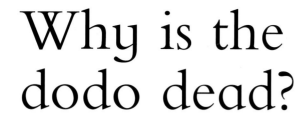

Dodos lived on the island of Mauritius in the Indian Ocean until they all died out in around 1680. Many were killed by hungry sailors who visited the island. The poor birds weren't used to hunters and were slow to escape because they couldn't fly.

The elephant bird was the largest bird to have ever lived. Its eggs were 200 times bigger than a chicken's egg! It died out around 300 years ago.

The dodo laid its eggs on the ground, making them easy pickings for hungry dogs or rats!

Which extinct animal looked half-horse, half-zebra?

Magnificent herds of quaggas
once roamed across
the grassy plains of
southern Africa.
But they were shot by
settlers for their unusual
skins and for their meat. So
many were killed that by
1883, there was not a single quagga left.

In England in the early
1800s, it was fashionable
to have quaggas pulling
your carriage.

The last Tasmanian tiger, or thylacine, died in
1936. It was a strange mixture of a beast. It
looked like it had the head of a wolf, the
stripes of a tiger, and the tail of a kangaroo!

How many insects are there?

So far we have found around one million different kinds of insects—more than any other type of creature. Yet many of them are at risk of extinction. If we continue destroying the places where these animals live, many will disappear forever—some before they've even been discovered.

The rare Queen Alexandra's bird wing butterfly lives in Papua New Guinea. But its forest home is being cleared.

There are so many insects that it is impossible to protect each and every one. The best way to save insects is to protect the places where they live.

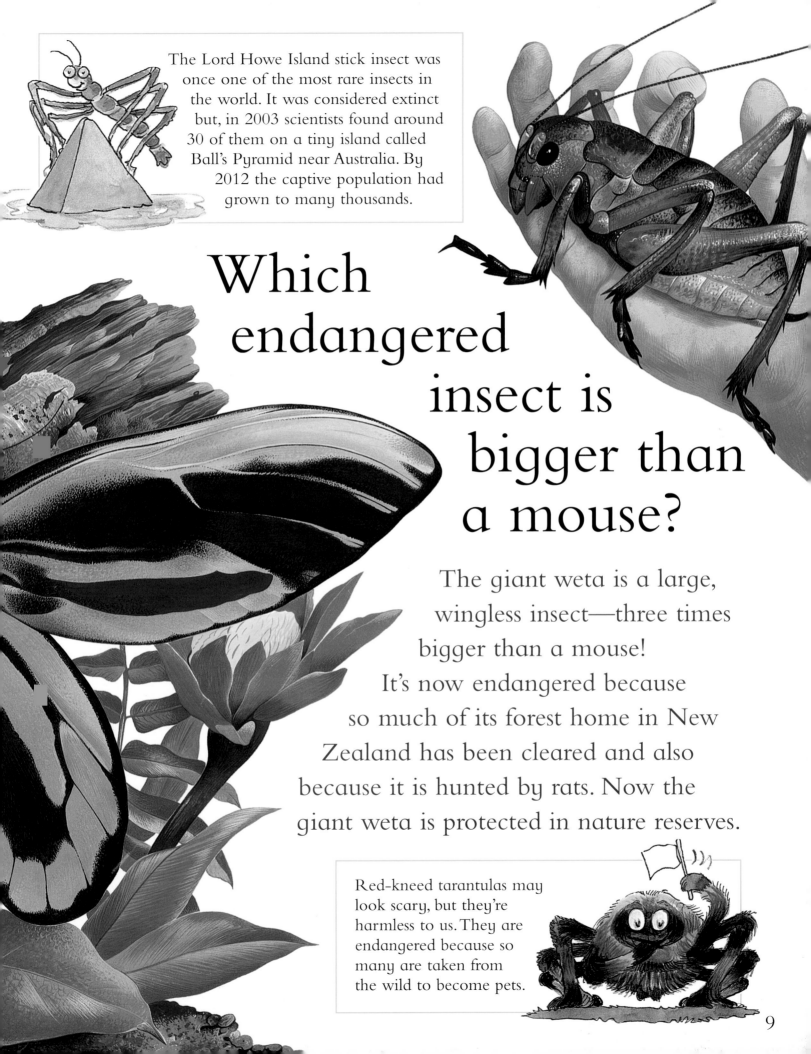

The Lord Howe Island stick insect was once one of the most rare insects in the world. It was considered extinct but, in 2003 scientists found around 30 of them on a tiny island called Ball's Pyramid near Australia. By 2012 the captive population had grown to many thousands.

Which endangered insect is bigger than a mouse?

The giant weta is a large, wingless insect—three times bigger than a mouse! It's now endangered because so much of its forest home in New Zealand has been cleared and also because it is hunted by rats. Now the giant weta is protected in nature reserves.

Red-kneed tarantulas may look scary, but they're harmless to us. They are endangered because so many are taken from the wild to become pets.

9

Why do animals like wetlands?

A boggy marsh or swamp provides a home and plenty of food for all kinds of different creatures. But wetlands are not being preserved. Many areas are drained to provide space for farms or housing. All wetland animals will be under threat if their homes continue to disappear.

Wetlands are good food stops for birds that fly long distances. They often stop over on long flights to rest or feed before continuing their journey.

Whooping crane

Snail kite

Beaver

Key deer

Leon Springs pupfish

Aquatic box turtle

American alligators were once hunted for their skins. By the 1960s they were endangered, and the hunting was stopped. Now their numbers are rising again.

Which orphans are fed by puppets?

In some Russian wetlands, people are caring for Siberian crane chicks who have no parents. These human "moms" wear sheets over their heads and puppets on their hands. The chicks think that they're being taken care of by real birds and are more likely to join a real flock when they grow up.

Wood stork

Schaus's swallowtail butterfly

Green heron

Marbled teal

Apache trout

American crocodile

Why are boats bad for manatees?

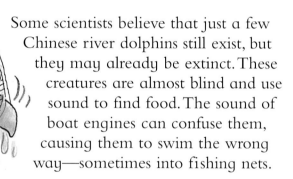

Manatees are gentle animals—they spend their life cruising along, grazing on sea grass. Unfortunately it's not only the manatees that enjoy a cruise. They share their waterways with fast-moving boats. Many manatees are cut by propeller blades, and the animals are getting rarer.

Some scientists believe that just a few Chinese river dolphins still exist, but they may already be extinct. These creatures are almost blind and use sound to find food. The sound of boat engines can confuse them, causing them to swim the wrong way—sometimes into fishing nets.

Where do sturgeon eggs go?

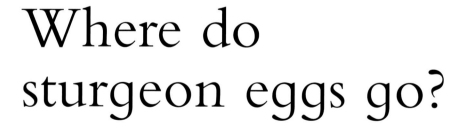

Every year sturgeons swim from the sea to the rivers where they were born to lay their eggs. Many don't make it—they are caught for their eggs. The eggs are sold as a luxury food called caviar.

Why should you keep olms a secret?

Animal collectors have taken so many olms from underground rivers and pools that they are now very rare. So when people find them in new, safe places, they should keep it a secret.

In a sea-life hospital in the U.S., injured manatees are given life jackets to wear. These help them to stay afloat while they get better.

How can fish make an eagle sick?

In Europe, river otters almost died out because their rivers were so polluted. But some of the rivers have been cleaned, and the otters are finally coming back.

The bald eagle was once close to extinction after its fish dinners had been poisoned by crop spray. The spray had washed off the land into lakes and entered the fish. Luckily the poison was banned, and the birds are thriving again.

13

Which endangered animal has a magic horn?

Rhinos live on the grasslands of Africa and Asia. It is against the law to hunt them, but some people still do. This is because they can get a lot of money for a rhino's horn. In some countries the horn is even considered magical. It is carved into dagger handles or ground up for medicine.

In some African nature reserves, the rangers catch the rhinos and cut off their horns. It doesn't hurt the rhinos, and hopefully it will stop the poachers from killing them.

The African pancake tortoise is endangered because so many are caught and sold as pets. In the wild it escapes from its enemies by hiding between rocks. It may fool other animals, but this trick doesn't work against hunters.

Where can you shoot elephants?

Elephants are endangered because so many are killed for their ivory tusks. In most places it is against the law to shoot them—except with a camera. The money the tourists pay to see the elephants can be spent on protecting these animals from poachers.

Like many grassland animals, the great bustard is becoming endangered as its home is turned into farmland. Cattle trample on the nests, and escaping birds often fly into overhead cables.

Which "extinct" animal returned to the wild?

Père David's deer were once extinct in the wild. The only ones left lived in zoos and parks. Luckily they were bred so successfully that now they are being returned to their grassland homes in northern China.

Why do orangutans need so many trees?

There are more kinds of trees and animals in the rainforests than in any other place. When the trees are cut down, all the living things in the forests are in danger.

Orangutans are rainforest animals that spend all their lives up in trees. When trees are cut down, spaces are left in the forest, and the orangutans can't swing around looking for food or places to sleep.

Which endangered animal is the shiest?

The shy okapi is so hard to find that scientists didn't know it existed until 1901! It's difficult to know exactly how many there are, but it's estimated that there are only 10,000 to 20,000 left in the wild.

Why is it bad luck to be an aye-aye?

Aye-ayes feed at night in the rainforests of Madagascar. Some of the people of that island think that aye-ayes bring bad luck, so they kill them. The animals are extremely rare, but in some places they are now protected.

Rainforest hunters have used poison from arrow-poison frogs on the tips of their arrows for hundreds of years. But now the frogs may become endangered because so many are being collected to sell as pets.

Which fox flies to its food?

The Rodrigues flying fox isn't a fox at all. It's a bat that lives on Rodrigues Island in the Indian Ocean. It eats fruit, so it needs many fruit trees. Most of its forest home has been cut down, and there are now only a few thousand of these bats left in the wild.

Why are polar bears still at risk?

Polar bears used to be hunted for their fur. That's stopped now, and the biggest threat to them is the planet overheating due to pollution in the air. If the Arctic ice melts, the bears won't be able to roam freely in search of food.

Why do seals get their fur dyed?

In some areas of the Canadian Arctic, the pups of harp seals are hunted for their pure white fur. People trying to protect the seals sometimes spray them with colored dye. It doesn't hurt the baby seals, but it makes their fur useless to the hunters.

In some areas, polar bears go into towns to scavenge for food. Hungry bears can be a danger to people. Some have to be shot, but most are just taken somewhere safer.

People almost hunted the musk ox to extinction until they realized they would make more money from its thick, soft fur than its meat. They stopped killing the ox and now comb it for its fur instead.

Which threatened whale has a unicorn's horn?

The narwhal is a kind of whale that lives in the Arctic seas. The male is hunted for his spiraled tusk that looks just like a unicorn's horn. If too many narwhals are taken, they may one day become extinct.

The only people who live in Antarctica are scientists working in research stations. There are no cities or towns. It is the last wilderness, and many believe it should stay that way.

KEEP OUT OF THE ANTARCTIC

GO AWAY

What's so "right" about the right whale?

The right whale got its name from the people who used to hunt it, the whalers. They said it was the right whale to catch because it gave plenty of useful whale bone and oil. So many were killed that it became endangered. Most hunting stopped in 1949, but the whales are still very rare.

The Inuit people of the Arctic still hunt right whales. They are allowed to because it is a part of their traditional way of life. Some people think this should be stopped, too.

Modern fishing boats can catch too many fish. If they continue taking so many, there'll come a day when all boats will trawl for the same few fish.

People have always been scared of great white sharks, but the sharks have more reason to be scared of us. Many are hunted every year, and their teeth and jaws are sold to make expensive trinkets.

At certain times large bands of crown-of-thorns sea stars get together to feast on coral. This may be because fishing boats are catching too many of the sea star's natural enemies.

Are there parks in the ocean?

We think of parks as being on land, but there are many in the sea. Many underwater parks and reserves have been made to protect the delicate coral reefs. The largest is the Great Barrier Reef off the coast of Australia. No one is allowed to harm the wildlife there.

Every year millions of sea creatures die because they get trapped in plastic garbage. Turtles often choke on plastic bags, mistaking them for yummy jellyfish.

When do parrots make bad pets?

Parrots make bad pets when they are born in the wild. Every year thousands of parrots are taken from their natural home to other countries in tiny, cramped boxes. Many die before they even get there; many more die right after.

An animal that is taken from its natural home is less likely to survive than one that is born and bred by people. If you want a pet, make sure that it isn't a wild animal.

Spix's macaws have been highly prized as pets. Today there are only around 85 left, but sadly none of them live in the wild. The last known wild Spix's macaw disappeared from northeast Brazil in 2000.

It is a good idea to find out how large your pet will become before you buy it. People are often surprised when the small pet they took home grows into a monster!

Who carries a chameleon in a suitcase?

Vacationers have been caught with chameleons in their suitcases. It's against the law to take endangered animals from one country to another. These people wanted to smuggle the lizards home.

Chimps, macaques, and tamarins are commonly owned by scientists, who test their new medicines on them. Some people say this has to be done to make sure that medicines are safe for humans. Others say it is cruel and should be stopped.

23

How could a bonfire save elephants?

The President of Kenya once set 13 tons (12 metric tonnes) of elephant tusks on fire, worth over $2,300,000. The tusks had been taken away from poachers. By burning them, Kenya was showing the world that it thought buying and selling ivory was wrong. It was hoping to persuade other countries to stop the trade in ivory and do more to protect elephants.

Who grabs coconut crabs?

Coconut crabs live on islands in the Pacific and Indian oceans. They grow to over 3 feet (1 meter) in length. They are hunted for food and made into souvenirs for tourists.

At 6 feet (1.8 meters) long, the Chinese giant salamander is the largest salamander in the world. So many people enjoy eating it that it has become endangered.

Why would leopards prefer to not be spotted?

Some people like to wear coats made out of beautiful, spotted leopard skins. Others hunt big cats because they find it an exciting sport. If the leopards had a say, they might let us know they'd prefer to have a plain skin that nobody wanted to wear— or else be harder to see in the first place.

Why do tigers need corridors?

In India, many tigers live in reserves and national parks where they are safe from hunters. The problem is that one park is often cut off from another. A "corridor" is a strip of forest linking two parks. Tigers can travel along it to find food or mates.

How does a possum cross the road?

The rare mountain pygmy possum of Australia uses a subway. After a road was built through its reserve, the males kept getting run over when they went to visit the females. Subways were built, and now they can cross the roads safely.

The Galápagos Islands in the Pacific Ocean are home to plants and animals not found anywhere else in the world. The islands have been turned into a huge national park, so all the wildlife there is protected.

Why are gorillas not to be sniffed at?

Mountain gorillas live in reserves high up in the Virunga Mountains in Africa. People can visit them, but the gorillas are not used to common human illnesses. They can die of flu. To protect the gorillas, visitors have to keep a safe distance.

There are probably less than 2,000 tigers left in India. They are protected by law, but poachers still kill them because their claws and bones can be sold to make medicine, and their fur also sells for a lot of money.

When do animals like going to the zoo?

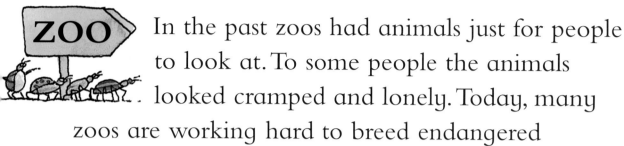

In the past zoos had animals just for people to look at. To some people the animals looked cramped and lonely. Today, many zoos are working hard to breed endangered animals, such as tamarins, in the hopes of returning them to the wild. If animals could talk, they might say they preferred this kind of zoo.

When do animals like leaving the zoo?

The last wild Arabian oryx was shot in 1972. Luckily a few were rescued before this and were kept in zoos. They bred well, and now a herd of around 1,000 or more roams the deserts of Oman.

Eighty years ago the golden hamster was almost extinct. Then one female and her 12 young were caught and allowed to breed in safety. Soon there were millions of them!

Which endangered animal is raised in a bucket?

Kemp's ridley turtle babies are being raised in special hatcheries in the U.S. and Mexico. In these buckets they are safe from seabirds and other hunters. When they are big enough to fend for themselves, they are put into the ocean.

Everyone thought the bridled nailtail wallaby, or flashjack, was extinct. Then a colony was discovered in 1973 near Dingo in eastern Australia. The area where they live is now protected.

Why do animals need us?

In most cases animals become endangered because of things that people do. Animals cannot speak, so they need some of us to speak up for them. And then they need us to stop doing the bad things we do, and save them.

Many people are helping animals in danger. If there's an oil spill, for example, teams work hard to clean the animals so that they can be returned to the wild.

Everyone can help save endangered animals. We can join groups that are trying to protect them. We can be careful about the things we buy, and we can take less from the natural world, pollute less, and recycle more.

Why do we need animals?

Some wild animals provide us with food, clothing, and other materials. If they disappear, we'll lose those things. Some animals may be useful to us in ways we don't know yet. Also animals make the world a beautiful and interesting place. If we lose them, it shows how little we care—for them, for the world, and for ourselves.

Many people believe we should save animals just because they exist. Animals have as much right to be on this planet as we do, and we should treat them with the same kindness that we would wish for ourselves.

Index

A

alligators 11
aye-ayes 17

B

beavers 10
butterflies 8, 11

C

chameleons 23
coconut crabs 25
coral 21
cranes 10, 11
crocodiles 11

D

deer 15
dinosaurs 4
dodos 6
dolphins 12

E

eagles 13
elephant birds 6
elephants 4, 15, 24
extinction 4, 6–7, 8, 13, 19, 22, 29

F

fishing 12, 20
  see also hunting
flying foxes 17
frogs 17
fur 18, 19, 27

G

giant salamanders 25
giant wetas 9
gorillas 27
grasslands 14, 15
great bustards 15
great white sharks 20

H

hamsters 29
hunting 5, 11, 12, 18, 19, 20, 25, 26

I

insects 8, 9

L

leopards 25

M

mammoths 4
manatees 12, 13
musk oxen 19

N

narwhals 19

O

okapis 16
olms 13
orangutans 16
oryx 28
otters 13

P

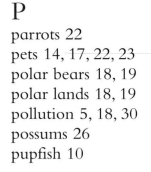

parrots 22
pets 14, 17, 22, 23
polar bears 18, 19
polar lands 18, 19
pollution 5, 18, 30
possums 26
pupfish 10

Q

quaggas 7

R

rainforests 16, 17
reserves 14, 21, 26, 27, 29
rhinos 14
right whales 20

S

seals 18
sea stars 21
snail kites 10
stick insects 9
sturgeons 12

T

tamarins 23, 28
tarantulas 9
Tasmanian tigers 7
teal 11
tigers 26, 27
tortoises 14
trout 11
turtles 10, 21, 29

W

wallabies 29
wetlands 10, 11

Z

zoos 15, 28